EXPLORATION

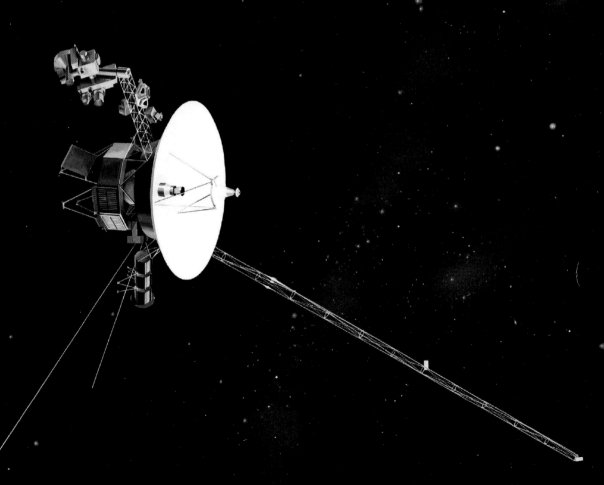

By S.L. Hamilton

VISIT US AT
WWW.ABDOPUBLISHING.COM

Published by ABDO Publishing Company, 8000 West 78th Street, Suite 310, Edina, MN 55439. Copyright ©2011 by Abdo Consulting Group, Inc. International copyrights reserved in all countries. No part of this book may be reproduced in any form without written permission from the publisher. A&D Xtreme™ is a trademark and logo of ABDO Publishing Company.

Printed in the United States of America, North Mankato, Minnesota.
112010
012011

PRINTED ON RECYCLED PAPER

Editor: John Hamilton
Graphic Design: Sue Hamilton
Cover Design: John Hamilton
Cover Photo: NASA/JPL
Interior Photos: All photos by NASA, except: pg 22 *Cassini* & *Huygens* artwork-NASA and European Space Agency/Images by D. Ducros; pg 26 Kepler telescope-Ball Aerospace & Technologies Corp.; pgs 28 (top) & 29 *Gaia*-ESA/Image by C. Carreau; pg 28 (bottom)-ESA/Image by Medialab.

Library of Congress Cataloging-in-Publication Data

Hamilton, Sue L., 1959-
  Exploration / S.L. Hamilton.
     p. cm. -- (Xtreme space)
  ISBN 978-1-61714-737-1
  1. Space probes--Juvenile literature. 2. Outer space--Exploration--Juvenile literature. 3. Manned space flight--Juvenile literature. I. Title.
  TL795.3.H36 2011
  919.9'204--dc22
                                2010041147

CONTENTS

Xtreme

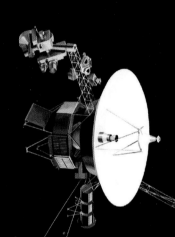

Voyager 1
space probe

Exploration

Humans want to explore and discover what exists in space. In 1977, NASA sent space probes *Voyager 1* and *2* to study Jupiter, Saturn, Uranus, Neptune, and Pluto. *Voyager 1* is now the farthest man-made object away from Earth.

Beginning

In 1961, President John F. Kennedy set
the American goal of "landing a man on
the Moon and returning him safely to the
Earth" by the end of the 1960's.

U.S. Space Exploration

Apollo 8's astronauts Frank Borman, William Anders, and James Lovell were the first men to see the far side of the Moon.

Apollo 8 **was the first manned flight into lunar orbit. It lifted off on December 21, 1968.**

EXPLORING

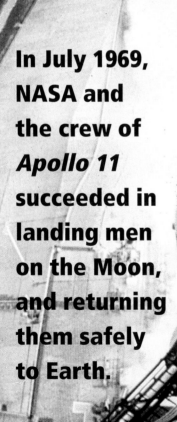

In July 1969, NASA and the crew of *Apollo 11* succeeded in landing men on the Moon, and returning them safely to Earth.

Apollo 11 launched on July 16, 1969. On board were astronauts Neil Armstrong, Michael Collins, and Edwin "Buzz" Aldrin.

THE MOON

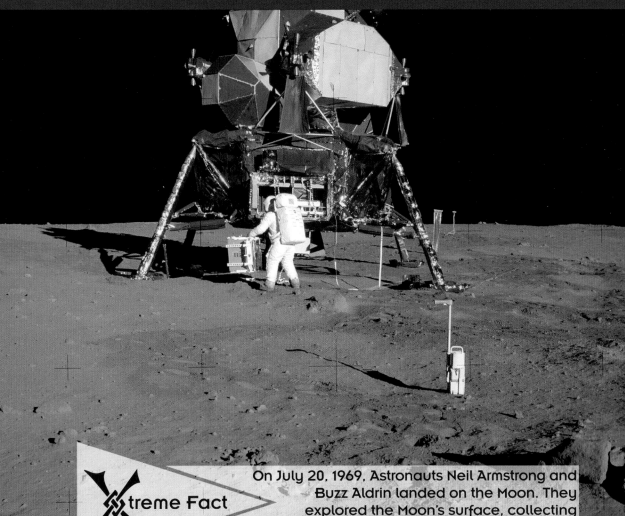

On July 20, 1969, Astronauts Neil Armstrong and Buzz Aldrin landed on the Moon. They explored the Moon's surface, collecting 47 pounds (21 kg) of lunar material.

Men on the Moon

Five more Apollo missions would land and explore the Moon. On December 14, 1972, *Apollo 17*'s Eugene "Gene" Cernan became the last man to walk on the Moon. American space exploration turned to new challenges.

Xtreme Quote

"As I take these last steps from the surface for some time to come, I'd just like to record that America's challenge of today has forged man's destiny of tomorrow." ~Gene Cernan

EXPLORING

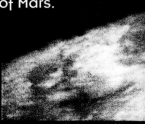

Mariner 4 photos of Mars.

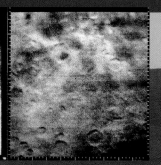

Opportunity Mars rover

For hundreds of years, people wondered what Mars looked like. The first close-up photos came from *Mariner 4* in 1965. Since then, scientists have explored Mars through flybys, orbiters, landers, and rovers. Beginning in 1997, Mars rovers traveled many miles across the planet. In 2001, the *Odyssey* orbiter began sending detailed information and pictures of the Red Planet.

The Mars rover *Opportunity* photographed part of itself.

MARS

This is part of a panorama photo made of more than 1,300 individual photos taken by *Opportunity*, a Mars exploration rover. It shows outcrop rocks, wind ripples, and small pebbles on the rim of Mars's Erebus crater.

Manned Mission to Mars

One of NASA's goals is to send astronauts to Mars. It would be a 2½-year mission. The trip takes about 6 months each way. Unmanned ships would take supplies and equipment to the planet. However, human safety is a big concern. The effects of radiation and long-term space travel are being studied. Robots will explore Mars until people can.

EXPLORING

Pioneer 10 was the first craft to reach Jupiter in 1973. Others followed, but NASA's *Galileo* spacecraft was made to study Jupiter. *Galileo* began orbiting our solar system's largest planet in December 1995. *Galileo* sent information and images of Jupiter and its moons for almost eight years.

Galileo launched from space shuttle *Atlantis* on October 18, 1989.

JUPITER AND ITS MOONS

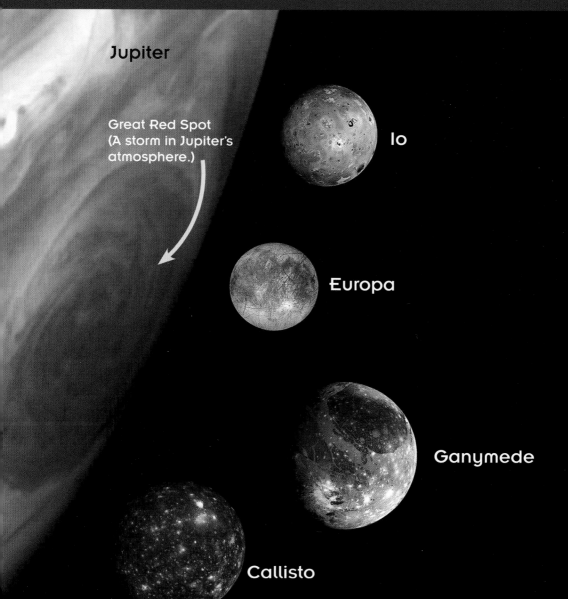

Jupiter

Great Red Spot
(A storm in Jupiter's
atmosphere.)

Io

Europa

Ganymede

Callisto

Jupiter's Moons

Four of Jupiter's 63 moons were explored by the *Galileo* spacecraft. Io (pronounced "EYE OH") has erupting volcanoes. Europa has dark strips crisscrossing its surface. Ganymede is the largest satellite in our solar system. It has an icy surface. Callisto has a very old surface, covered with craters.

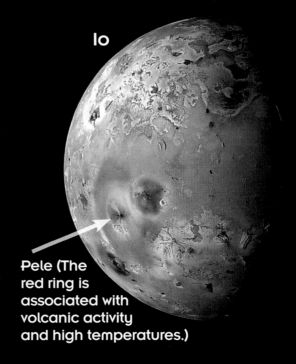

Io

Pele (The red ring is associated with volcanic activity and high temperatures.)

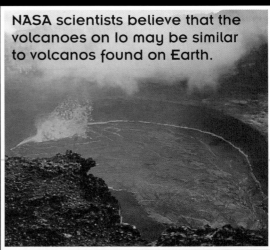

NASA scientists believe that the volcanoes on Io may be similar to volcanos found on Earth.

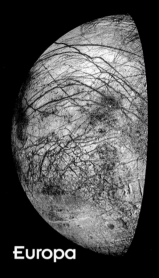

Europa

An 87-mile-wide (140-km) impact scar on Europa. It formed after a mountain-sized asteroid or comet slammed into Europa's surface.

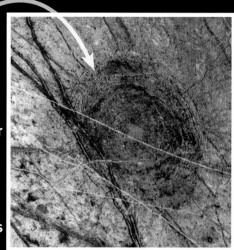

Ganymede

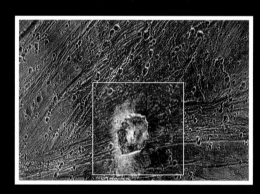

Ganymede's Kittu crater is seen in nearly true color. The photo was taken by *Galileo* cameras.

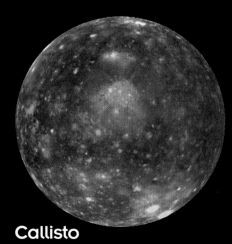

Callisto

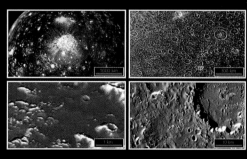

Close-up images of Callisto's icy surface with many deep craters.

EXPLORING

Saturn, with its familiar rings, has long interested people. On October 15, 1997, the *Cassini* orbiter was launched to explore Saturn and its rings and moons.

SATURN AND ITS MOONS

On July 1, 2004, *Cassini* carefully moved through two of Saturn's rings. It slid into place to become the first craft to orbit the planet.

Cassini's wide-angle camera shot this image of Saturn's clouds in 2007. The swirling atmosphere looks like a piece of Earth sandstone.

Exploring Titan

The *Cassini* orbiter carried with it the *Huygens* probe. On January 14, 2005, the *Huygens* probe descended and landed on Titan, Saturn's largest moon. Among *Huygens*'s many discoveries, it has found Earth-like rocks and lakes of ethane and methane.

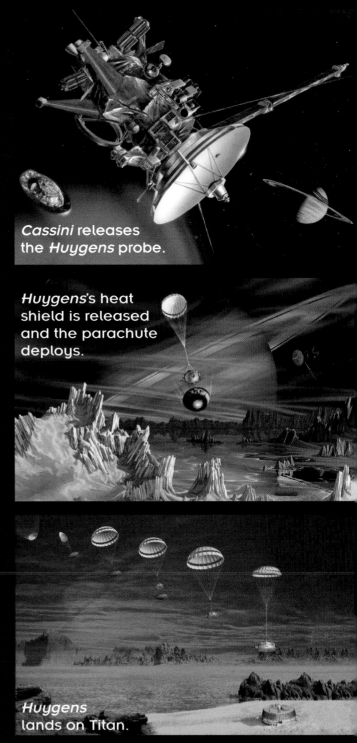

Cassini releases the *Huygens* probe.

Huygens's heat shield is released and the parachute deploys.

Huygens lands on Titan.

Rocks on Titan.

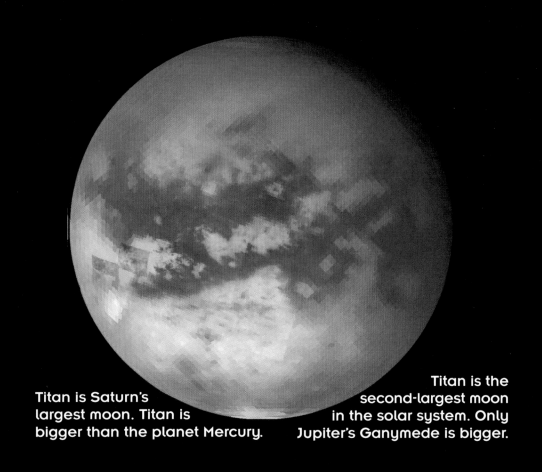

Titan is Saturn's largest moon. Titan is bigger than the planet Mercury.

Titan is the second-largest moon in the solar system. Only Jupiter's Ganymede is bigger.

Aerial Views of Titan around the *Huygens* Landing Site

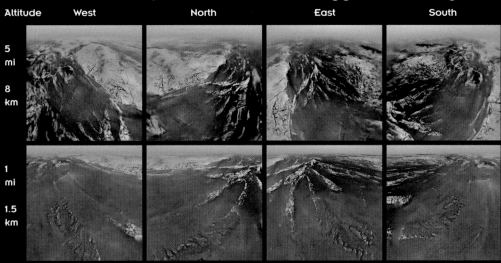

Altitude	West	North	East	South
5 mi 8 km				
1 mi 1.5 km				

SEARCHING FOR

Planet Quest and Terrestrial Planet Finder are programs whose mission is to find planets similar to Earth. Scientists search the universe using telescopes and space probes.

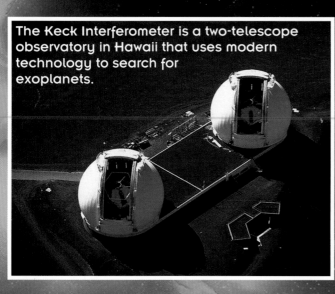

The Keck Interferometer is a two-telescope observatory in Hawaii that uses modern technology to search for exoplanets.

ANOTHER EARTH

An exoplanet is a planet that orbits a star other than our Sun. Many exoplanets have been discovered so far.

Kepler Mission

How many Earthlike planets are in our own Milky Way galaxy? Launched on March 6, 2009, the *Kepler* spacecraft and telescope is being used to explore and find habitable planets. Earthlike planets would be orbiting stars like our Sun.

The Kepler telescope was built to study one area of the universe for 3½ to 4 years.

Milky Way Galaxy

Kepler Search Space

← 3,000 light years →

Sagittarius Arm

⊕ **Sun**

Orion Spur

Perseus Arm

First Five Planet Discoveries
Made with First 43 Days of Data

Mission Time

Mass (Earth masses)

- 5b
- 6b
- 8b
- 7b
- 4b

Jupiter
Saturn
Neptune
Uranus

Venus ♀   ⊕ Earth

Mars

○ Kepler Exoplanets
■ Habitable Planets

Orbital Distance (AU)

Mapping The

Due to launch in 2012, the *Gaia* spacecraft's mission will be to map the Milky Way galaxy. Space exploration adds to our knowledge of our planet's history.
It also lets people know what is waiting to be discovered and explored.

MILKY WAY

Gaia has a deployable sun shield to protect its state-of-the-art optics from temperature changes as it scans space.

THE

Ethane

A colorless, odorless gas used as a fuel on Earth. On Saturn's moon Titan, there are lakes of liquid ethane.

Flyby

When a craft flies near and passes over a specific object, such as a spacecraft flying by a planet.

Lander

A spacecraft designed to land on and study a planet or moon.

Methane

A colorless, odorless gas used as a fuel on Earth. On Saturn's moon Titan, there are lakes of liquid methane.

Milky Way

The spiral galaxy containing Earth and all the planets, stars, and other objects that orbit our Sun.

National Aeronautics and Space Administration (NASA)

A United States government agency started in 1958.

GLOSSARY

NASA's goals include space exploration, as well as increasing people's understanding of Earth, our solar system, and the universe.

Orbiter

A spacecraft designed to stay in orbit around a planet or moon, and study that object. An orbiter does not land on the object it is studying.

Probe

A device designed to explore and obtain information about a planet, moon, or other object.

Rover

A manned or unmanned vehicle designed to travel across and study the landscape of a planet or moon.

Space Shuttle

America's first reusable space vehicle. NASA built five orbiters: *Columbia, Challenger, Atlantis, Discovery,* and *Endeavour.* Two shuttles and their crews were destroyed in accidents: *Challenger* (1986) and *Columbia* (2003).

INDEX